Contents

Words printed in **bold** appear in the glossary.

As good as anyone else

On 15 January 1929, the Reverend King had some good news to tell people at his church in Atlanta, in the southern United States. He had a new son! He and his wife named their child Martin Luther.

As a boy, Martin loved to listen to his grandmother read from the Bible and to play games with his sister and brother.

The house in Atlanta where Martin was born.

Even more, he enjoyed playing with the children of the local shopkeeper. This was very unusual in Atlanta, because Martin was black and his friends were white.

Black people first came to the United States as **slaves**, but now they were free people. Even so, many white Americans, especially in the South, did not want to mix with black people. They believed in **segregation**.

When Martin was growing up, black people in the South had to eat in different cafés from white people.

When Martin started school, he was surprised to find that his friends went to a different school. They were no longer allowed to play with him. He also saw that black people were treated with less respect than white people. This kind of treatment is called **discrimination**.

Martin was hurt by this treatment. He told his mother how he felt. She replied, 'Don't let it make you feel you are not as good as white people. You are as good as anyone else, and don't you forget it!'

In the segregated South there were separate public washrooms for white and black people.

Freedom in the North

Martin loved reading and enjoyed his days at school. When he was fifteen he won a place on a special course for clever black children, at Morehouse College in Atlanta. When Martin

started at the college, he knew he wanted to do something to help black people, but he was not sure what. Eventually, he decided to become a church **minister**. He hoped this would help him to bring change.

In 1948, Martin left Morehouse as a **Baptist** minister. He later decided to study at Boston University, in the northern state of Massachusetts. In northern states blacks had greater freedom than in the South. But even there, some whites did not treat them fairly.

Martin enjoyed his life in Boston very much. He made lots of friends. He also met Coretta Scott, a beautiful young woman

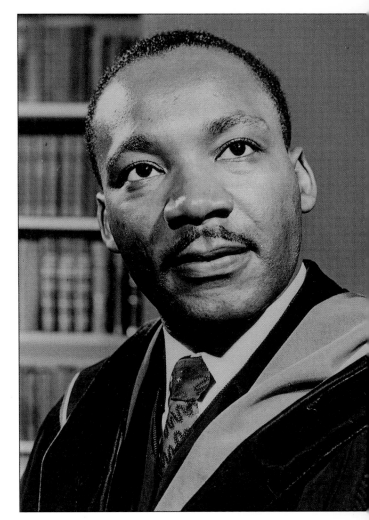

Martin posed proudly after finishing his studies at Boston University.

from Alabama who was studying to become a concert singer. He fell in love with her and asked her to marry him.

9

Martin and his wife Coretta with three of their four children.

Martin and Coretta were married in 1953. They returned to the South, where Martin found a job as minister at a church in Montgomery, Alabama.

After their first child was born they looked forward to a happy, peaceful life.

Time for action

The Kings' peaceful life ended on 1 December 1955. Mrs Rosa Parks, a black women travelling home after a hard day at work, refused to give up her seat on a Montgomery city bus to a white person. The bus driver called the police. Mrs Parks was arrested.

Black people were used to being treated as **second-class citizens** on the city buses, but this time the bus company had gone too far.

Black leaders became very angry. They decided to **demonstrate**. They wanted to stop this unfair treatment of black passengers.

A **committee** was set up and Martin joined it. The committee organized a **boycott** of the Montgomery buses.

'Don't use the buses,' the committee urged. 'Take a taxi, or share a ride, or walk.'

Right *Martin (centre) shakes hands with his lawyer after he was found guilty of helping to organize a bus boycott.*

Even as a child, Martin had hated fighting. When he was at university, he had read about the Indian leader Mahatma Gandhi. Gandhi had used peaceful **protests**, such as boycotts and marches, to bring great changes in India. Now Martin urged black people to use the same peaceful methods to bring about change in the United States.

Although Martin's methods were peaceful, his family faced many dangers because of his actions. He received nasty phone calls from angry whites. Twice he was arrested, and later

released. Worst of all, someone threw a bomb into his house. Luckily, no one was hurt.

Black people continued to protest for nearly a year. Eventually, the United States **Supreme Court** decided that the Alabama bus laws were **illegal**. Black people could now sit wherever they liked on the buses.

Angry whites burned a cross in front of Martin's house to protest against his work.

Freedom rider

After the bus boycott, Martin continued to preach at his church. He also worked very hard for black people. Finally, Martin realized that he had to choose between his job as a minister and his work as a **civil rights** leader.

It was a hard choice, but at the end of 1959 Martin decided to leave his church. 'History has thrust something upon me which I cannot turn away,' he said.

In 1960, black students all over the South began to

visit **lunch-counters** in stores and restaurants. They would ask, politely but firmly, to be served. These protests were called **sit-ins**. The aim was to end segregation at the counters. Martin joined the students in their sit-ins.

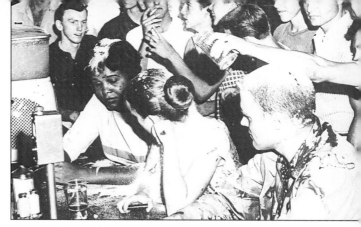

Black students held sit-ins at lunch-counters, to try to make them open to everyone.

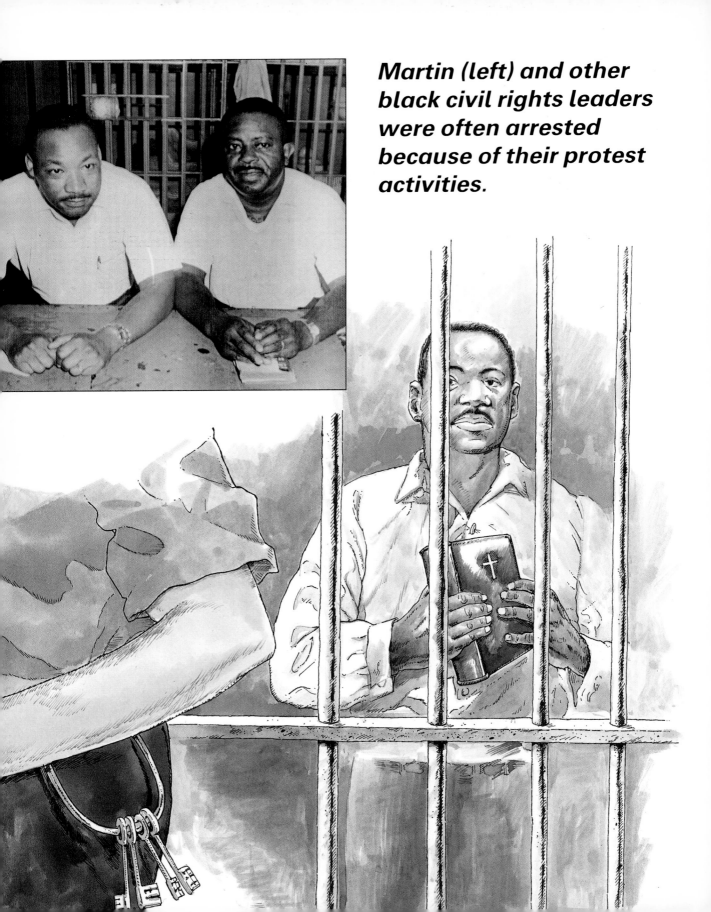

Martin (left) and other black civil rights leaders were often arrested because of their protest activities.

Black 'Freedom Riders' sitting in the 'Whites only' section of a bus station waiting room.

When a group of students was arrested in Atlanta, Martin was arrested too. He was given a very harsh sentence – four months in a prison where black people were treated very badly. An important **politician**, John F Kennedy, who was hoping to become President of the United States, heard of the sentence. He was able to get Martin freed.

Martin went straight back to work. He joined the 'Freedom Riders', a group of black students who travelled on buses throughout the South. They did this to demonstrate for civil rights for black people.

'I have a dream'

To Martin, the city of Birmingham, Alabama, was 'the most thoroughly segregated city in America'. He made up his mind to change this. In 1963, he organized sit-ins and marches in the city. The Birmingham police dragged many black protesters off to prison. Martin was one of them.

He was set free after a week and went back to organizing marches. In one march, he was joined by thousands of black children. They marched in the hope that they would grow up in a country where blacks had the same rights as whites. Once again, the police moved in. Many children were arrested.

Martin organized and led many civil rights marches.

These events were shown on television in many different countries. People all over the world saw how badly American blacks were treated. Many Americans were ashamed of their country. They wanted things to change.

In August 1963 a quarter of a million people, both black and white, went on a march to Washington, DC, the United States' **capital**. Martin had written a speech. But he put down his notes and spoke straight from his heart. 'I have a dream,' he said, 'that my four little children will be judged, not by the colour of their skin, but by the content of their character. I have a dream today!'

In 1964, Martin Luther King won the Nobel Peace Prize.

Martin's words were heard around America and the world. A year later he was given the **Nobel Peace Prize.** As he accepted the prize, he said he looked forward to 'the bright daylight of peace and brotherhood'. But he knew there was still a long way to go.

Martin in front of the crowds during the huge march to Washington, DC, in 1963.

Long hot summer

Martin continued to try to organize peaceful marches. But black people were becoming angry. They were tired of waiting for things to change. Soon **race riots** broke out in many cities all over the United States.

Many black people were very poor. Their homes were in poor areas. Martin believed the only way to stop the riots was to end this **poverty**.

In 1966 he moved with his family to the northern

city of Chicago. There he tried to help blacks improve the places where they lived. But in spite of his efforts, riots broke out during the long hot summer of 1967.

Right *Martin worked to keep the issue of black rights in the news.*

In 1968, Martin decided to travel to Memphis, Tennessee, to march with some black workers. When he arrived in Memphis, Martin told people, 'I don't know what will happen to me now, but it really doesn't matter . . . I have seen the **promised land**.'

The next evening, 4 April 1968, Martin was standing on the balcony of his hotel in Memphis with a friend. Suddenly a shot rang out from across the street. Martin Luther King lay dead. The shot was fired by a white man, James Earl Ray.

After Martin Luther King was killed, serious riots broke out in many cities.

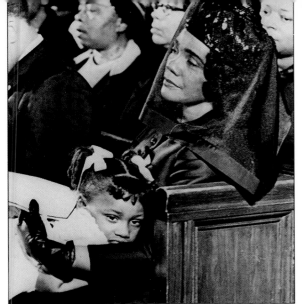

Many black people were so angry at Martin's death that there were serious riots in more than a hundred cities across the United States.

Mrs King comforts her daughter at Martin's funeral.

Free at last

On Martin Luther King's gravestone are the words 'Free at last'. Thanks to his work, much has changed for black Americans. However, black people still have a long way to go before they can say that they are truly free.

Martin believed in the power of peaceful protest to bring about change. Many people continue to work peacefully to help make his dream come true for black people everywhere.

Date chart

1929 15 January Martin Luther King is born in Atlanta, Georgia.

1944 Enters Morehouse College, Atlanta.

1948 Leaves Morehouse College as a Baptist minister.

1953 Marries Coretta Scott.

1954 Becomes minister at a Baptist church in Montgomery, Alabama.

1955 Receives his degree from Boston University.

1956 Leads the black people's boycott of the Montgomery city buses.

1959 Leaves his church to become a civil rights leader.

1960 Joins the 'Freedom Riders'.

1963 Organizes a campaign of sit-ins and marches in Birmingham, Alabama. Delivers his 'I have a dream . . .' speech at a march in Washington, DC.

1964 Awarded the Nobel Peace Prize.

1966 Moves to Chicago, Illinois, to help fight poverty among blacks.

1968 4 April Killed in Memphis, Tennessee.

Glossary

Baptist Belonging to the Baptist Church. Baptism is a Christian religion.

Boycott A type of protest whereby people refuse to buy certain goods or use a particular service. In Montgomery, black people refused to use the buses. This meant the buses lost money.

Capital The city that is the centre for a country's government.

Civil rights The things that people think everyone should have, such as the power to vote and being able to live under fair laws.

Committee A group of people chosen to look into and act on a particular matter.

Demonstrate To protest about something by making a show in public.

Discrimination Treating people differently, usually worse, because they are different in some way. For example, black people may be discriminated against simply because of their colour.

Illegal Against the law.

Lunch-counter In the United States, a kind of snack bar.

Minister The religious leader of a church.

Nobel Peace Prize A prize given every year to someone who has made an important contribution to peace. A Nobel Prize is considered the world's finest honour.

Politician A person who is involved in deciding

how a country is run. For example, politicians are members of the Senate in the United States, or of Parliament in Britain.

Poverty Lack of money.

Promised land A term that comes from the Bible and means a place where people expect to have a better life.

Protest A public way of showing that you do not agree with something. People who hold protests are called protesters.

Race riots Fighting between people of different races.

Second-class citizens People who are treated badly because they are thought of as less important.

Segregation A system of laws and customs that keeps people of different races apart. For example, they must use separate restaurants and sit in different parts of a bus.

Sit-ins Protests whereby people sit in a public building and refuse to leave.

Slaves People who are owned by someone else and forced to work without pay.

Supreme Court The highest court of law in the United States.

Books to read

Martin Luther King by Nigel Richardson (Hamish Hamilton, 1983)

Martin Luther King by Nigel Hunter (Wayland, 1985)

Index

Picture acknowledgements
The publishers would like to thank the
following: Camera Press cover and
frontispiece (Karsh of Ottawa), 4 (W.
Hamilton), 9 (Karsh of Ottawa); Peter
Newark's Western Americana 6;
Photri 7, 21; Popperfoto 18, 19;
Topham 10, 13, 17, 22, 23, 25, 26;
Wayland Picture Library 15 (United
Press International), 27 (Associated
Press).